As the World Winds Flow

As the World Winds Flow

Carroll Blair

Aveon Publishing Company

Copyright © 2017 by Carroll Blair

All rights reserved. No part of this book may be reproduced, or transmitted in any form or by any means, electronic or mechanical, including photocopy, recording, or by any information storage and retrieval system without prior permission of the publisher.

ISBN: 978-1-936430-31-4

Library of Congress Control Number
2016916350

Aveon Publishing Co.
P.O. Box 380739
Cambridge, MA 02238-0739 USA

Also by Carroll Blair

Grains of Thought
Facing the Circle
Reel to Real
Shifting Tides
Reaches
Out of Silence
Quarter Notes
By Rays of Light
Into the Inner Life
Gnosis of the Heart
Soul Reflections
Beneath and Beyond the Surface
Of Courage and Commitment
For Today and Tomorrow
In Meditation
Sightings Along the Journey
Through Desert's Fire
Offerings to Pilgrims
Human Natures
(Of Animal and Spiritual)
Atoms from the Suns of Solitude
Colors of Devotion
Voicings
Through the Shadows

For Marjorie Blair

In Memoriam

Contents

Part I

In Passing	17
A Moment's Wonder	18
Keeping It Together	19
Ear Shot	20
Two Sides of Nature	21
Over-Sight	22
Each Day and Night	23
Of Distance and Relation	24
On a Sunday Morning	25
Goading the Hour	26
Solo Invitation	27
Ground Zero	28
Field Day	29
Cross Fashion	30
Without Cover	31
A Science Aim	32
The Bizarreness of Quantum Physics	33
Where Freedom Sings Free	34
Understanding	35
Like Something Other	36
Behind the Veil	37
Raising Stakes	38
A Beauty	39
Driving It Home	40
Adding Steps	41

Something Better	42
Increase of Power	43
Artist	44
New Light	45
The Great Intelligence	46
Most Creative Paradise	47
Spirit at Its Best	48
An Assessment	49
On the Verge Of	50
And of Humankind	52
Leaving Themselves Behind	53
Landscapes	54
Side Roads and Back Roads	55
Never a Chorus	56
The Way It Is	57
A Difference	58
When Disposed to Thought	59
Waiting to Delight	60
No Matter What	61
Resurrection	62

Part II

On a Hill	65
Like a Symphony	66
Witness to Perfection	67
Nature Jazz	68
To Take It All In	69
The Poet's Birth of Awakening	70
As Ancient Palms	71
When Crowded and Empty	72
Oceans	73
Thrill of a Youth Time	74
Just Thought to Mention	75
Touch of Seasons	76
Looking Up	77
Still Light There	78
Sometimes Alone	79
Different Measure	80
Before the Flow	81
So Much Left Out	82
The Baby Shower	83
Odds to Wonder	84
Too Much to Handle	85
Of Birth and Death	86
No Longer Step	87
Well Well Well	88
With Minds Closed	89
Killing Santa Claus	90
Pet Watch	91
Complacent Trance	92

The Perilous Wait	93
CHANGE	94
Over the Rest	95
Empty Beneath the Sun	96
Ripe for the Breaking	97
Still Searching For	98
For Ray	99
Good Time Benny	100
Fantasy Meets Fantasy	101
Air Speak	102
Not a Note	103
Once Budding King	104
Winking at Shadows	105
Suicides	106
Something Lost	107
Of Lives Taken	108
Before the Parting	109
The Finest $ Can Buy	110
Grand Misunderstanding	111
Only Man	112
Up or Down	113
Dead of Life	114
No Other	115
Offering to the Young	116
Saving Grace	117
Words	118
An Answer	119
A Place for One	120
Cannot Erase	121

I

In Passing

Coming in out of the sun, followed by wind
and flecks of earth, the air from inside and out
joined by the opening of a door birthing the
thought of a bird needing to get the feel of
the nest, then the feel of the sky on its wings
and that of a branch swaying beneath its grip
at the end of its virgin flight, then back to the
Now at hand, all thought shifting to the rooms
and quiet spaces of the abode newly entered,
there before eyes that have looked so far and
seen so much, gazing from the body of one
just satisfied to be in quarters not accompanied
by a company of more than one, present in
an enclosure of peace and calm without
intrusion of before or after, giving refuge
to a lone seeker who's of the mind to be
grateful for this gift —

A Moment's Wonder

A man and two dogs are walking
on the street and it is not clear
if the man is walking the dogs
or the dogs are walking the man
and seems to not matter to either
and matters not to me

But just for a moment   I wondered

Keeping It Together

The morning came in with the clearest
of skies and wafts of mild winds though
within the hour the sunlight disappeared
and the winds suddenly rose, surging to
a velocity of speed and power roaring
with intensity, bringing rain and thunder
along for the ride which lasted for more
than a while then the winds relaxed,
diminishing to their prior state and the
rain took its leave and the sunlight
reappeared as pretty as you please

This New England weather of the
mercurial [so unpredictable] somehow
keeping it all together —

Ear Shot

Stepping out onto the sidewalk
taking their evening stroll before
dark, a couple converse as they
pass by a house occupied by one
and their voices sound muffled
through the walls, and the birds
answer in sound heard sweet and
clear as if there were no walls

Two Sides of Nature

On a warm and sunlit day nearing the dawn
of summer, a party of guests sat under a canopy
on the back lawn of a suburban residence
viewing pictures of a family of swans on a park
pond taken by one of the gathering; the parents
bordering their offspring numbering four
between them, creating a lateral union of a
symmetry complementing the natural beauty
of the environment; still-shots of peaceful motion
on tranquil waters, the showing of swans
and other pictures of greenery and gardens of a
parkland and a backdrop of sky and sunset enjoyed
by the gathering sitting comfortably in their lawn
chairs, while in the midst of the carefree moment
a hawk suddenly appeared, approaching with deadly
purpose, swift and sure of its target, taking prey
from the largest tree on the grounds near the front
of the address away from all but one of the guests,
the branches violently shaking at the point of attack
sending leaves in flight with sounds of screeching
terror, the hawk fast departing with a bird of another
species held in its talons, fading back into the sky . . .
an exhibition of the life-and-death struggle ever
in play even when removed from the heart of the
wild, witnessed by one who chose to leave his chair
for a walk around the yard seconds before the killing
attack, moved to reflect on the raw brutality of the
event unbeknownst to the rest of the party of guests
emitting sounds of laughter and mirthful chatter,
reposed and far away (in mind more than in body)
from this sobering side of Nature —

Over – Sight

A cloud drifts by overhead
of a white circumference bright
all around with a mixture of
gray and black between the white
darkening its center, the cloud
moving on as life goes along
with opposites held together
doing existence in the round
and round of it all . . .

Each Day and Night

People in numbers too vast to be counted
dine together without knowing one another,
without conversing with one another, dining
in restaurants in silence to most present though
the air be filled with a mixture of words and
laughter and other sounds familiar in gatherings
of pairs and trios and parties of four or more,
discoursing amongst themselves but not the
others under the same roof, seated on different
chairs at different tables, eating different meals
enjoying by different degrees, different company
to come and go, leaving the chairs empty and
tables full to be cleared for the next arrivals,
to fill the air with similar sounds, though the
particulars ever different —

Of Distance and Relation

Our distance from the sun changes moment to
moment, changing the same for everyone, yet also
different depending on where you are lying or
sitting or standing, walking or running, the earth
forever turning toward and away from the sun
at the same instant while orbiting around it, constantly changing our position and distance-relation
to it as the sun orbits nothing, holding its position
in our solar system though being part of another perennial change of distance involving every entity in
the universe happening at every second, though the
change here different in kind from that of the above,
distancing star from star and galaxy from galaxy,
further separating by way of inflation; celestial bodies
held in their structure, but the expansion of space
ever moving them apart — and how one can feel
at times is similar to this cosmic phenomenon . . .
held in one's life [to one's being] as forces of Life
seem to be creating more distance between lives,
pushing them farther away from one another
though bodies within range of sight, idle or
moving about in space and time —

On a Sunday Morning

Sitting before his breakfast pondering
the universe, thinking about galaxies many
light years away, about cosmic matter
now exploding in a heat of violence not to
be fully comprehended by the imagination . . .
the physics professor lost in reverie of
worlds far away as another coffee is poured
with children running in and out of the
kitchen and around the table, the table
holding its illusion of stillness

Goading the Hour

Prisoners there were, in turbans
dressed to shock with verbal
photographs hung from tongue
to vest, goading the hour for more
than was asked for which had its
own kind of beauty matched by
cracked celery in paper cups
filling in for the flowers held up
in some chain of evidence for all
the blind to see —

Solo Invitation

Startled by a flash of awakening
catching the evening force, coursing
its way to invention with primal cunning;
campfires rise in the distance lighting
the trail of nomads shunned by a star
fixed to wanderings no knight of the
landing has yet to follow, clad in
branes of happenstance wrung through
anonymous ties, facing the hourglass
toward a mountain of white sand
for a change of grace, wide open
amid the roar of thunder —

Ground Zero

A call for redemption forcing revision
from the face of history, its makeovers
uncurtained losing the feint of its mystery
and colorings of tradition, splicing circle
upon circle shattered by the order of a
king's blood ransom ready for the sword
swallowers and fire-eaters to finish, then
off like lovers not taking their time
rounding full circle, breaking the barrier
to Start —

Field Day

The bells rang early that day
chiming from the tower without
warning, sending shopkeepers from
their homes entering the streets
of lost earnings keeping the
children company for a while,
lost in games of cruelty . . .
spoons scraped the dirt whirled
from crates of needless goods
set above glass cages borne by
bartered clay open through times
of promise betrayed, sighing between
the blows of whistles from a train
never coming into view . . .

Cross Fashion

A motion severed from the body of its fate
shaking stones from the hooves of zebras
slowing down for the lion six months old —
A sense of giving in the herd (oh what's
come over them [!]) . . . rumors abound by
the cause for where they are going unseen,
untested, where the rain falls short on torrid
lands, crossing in fashion known by heart
to those who live without one —

Without Cover

Behold the rising slipping into something
less comfortable moving without cover,
refusing a climate of change and silent
go-betweens clearing scenes through a
fog of perennial endings and currents
of new beginnings, split in multiple primes
crouching in innocence before sciences
haunted by a loss of peace reaching for
a second chance and the promise of no
surprise, trailing a saint's passage through
a marsh of hear-what-I-say/mean/say
waving the story of forgiveness, knowing
for the first time what the all of tender means —

A Science Aim

... learning how the world works
to better work the world

The Bizarreness of Quantum Physics

— like the existence of all the pieces to a puzzle that doesn't exist

Where Freedom Sings Free

. . . in the corners of night spells
drawn to light that no one can see
creating doubt in Dream and
Life and Being

Understanding

— as when you get to an ending
and still don't understand until
returning to the beginning
the answer being there all along
but not revealed until back to
the end of the turnaround —

Like Something Other

Sometimes life is like standing on a
floor but feels like standing on a wall
and the vertical becomes the horizontal
and the air becomes something else,
something other-than and the room
waves silent in its reconfiguration

                 . . . . sometimes

Behind the Veil

Behind the veil of Somewhere
After, voices flicker as a flame
that can't be dreamed . . .

Bodies fade like gondolas
slipping into twilight
decorous as a calendar's
gaze

Raising Stakes

Turning from remembrance passing by
what once was a sea powered by batteries
lighting runways for unsteady dreams
carrying cargo from faraway places
that cannot be traced or returned to,
housing lost voyagers that truly don't
wish to be found, yearning for pastoral
calm amid trials of lunacies bound by
centuries holding passports to mines of
disillusionment, waiting for the savior
in his chariot believing in dough and
Pillsbury skies

A Beauty

There is a beauty in life's all-of-a-sudden-
just-didn't-see-it-coming ways however
unsettling or disturbing, sending shock
waves through parts of the world
(sometimes the whole world) turning
things upside down and around this way
and that, and in the mix of the shakeup,
corrosives being dispersed [broken up]
in the human soul and heart that need to
be removed [flushed out] to make way
for better days, bringing opportunity for
fresh winds of creativity and possibility
ready to move the brave and ready to
new ventures of the human experience,
to take it somewhere else [to an elsewhere
of new frontiers] finding the way to
better ways, engaged in the discovery
of what makes it all worthwhile —

Driving It Home

Sometimes the day comes at you like a
hard line drive and there's nothing you
can do but step into it, meet it straightaway
and not let its power escape you or have it
roll over you or past you, refusing it the
option of leaving you ineffective (not in
the game), not stepping up to the force
coming your way, losing another chance
to take it and give it back in spades, hence
meeting the day's power with power of
your own, driving it hard and true . . .

[driving it home]

Adding Steps

The way life will go [will shake] one day
to the next is anyone's guess [like the
oceans' tides, we've no control over this]
but when not going well or turning a better
way for us, we can still join the dance and add
a counterstep or more [yes, this we can do]
to [if nothing else] make it interesting or
leastwise enough to keep us from doing what
falls to the trivial and learn a few new steps
[new moves], a new groove, perhaps, as we
discover how much of what goes on between
life and us is really up to us as to how it is
received and how we respond to its ebbs
and flows which no one controls or leads,
though we can make something or do some-
thing with them in the space that is ours
to step and dance as we please —

Something Better

People are fascinated by things that
are not of this world, captivated by
the existence of alien phenomena like
asteroids and meteorites, moondust
and moon rocks and red soil from the
planet Mars, and other extraterrestrial
substances made known to humankind
by space vehicles launched from Earth
to explore other worlds . . . many would
pay a high price, exert great efforts to
possess samples of these materials when
they could have something more valuable
by far yet rarely realized in this world
but here now in this world [available to
this world], to be experienced in this life
[in this world] by those who connect
with the eternal of their lives, the
source behind all there is of Being
and the mystery that lies beyond it —
the deathless power within —

Increase in Power

Deserving is life of a great deal of thought . . .
and something required if the best of its
gifts, one is to be worthy of . . . yes —
thought, added in increments as one goes
along yet also pausing at times to give it
a whole lot, thus adding power to a life,
growing in light and understanding,
manifesting a journey more accomplished
for having given the time and effort to
indulge a probing curiosity, feeding a
sense of wonder for the glorious mystery
that has been given the name of Life —

Artist

Ready to pick up the thread
the thread of his force, the
 thread of his power
the thread that can be lost
 but never broken

New Light

Influences of a life
finding their way to
one another, creating
a new Influence
adding new light
to the world

The Great Intelligence

. . . like a revolving coil ever
taking in and turning out
exploring the outer and the
inner, one unable to profoundly
be known without the other,
winding it all together in
a balance of discord and
harmony that mirrors
the structure of life

Most Creative Paradise

Spirit . . . dwelling in the sphere
of Nowhere and Everywhere . . .
held to nothing, open to everything . . .
the most creative paradise
there will ever be —

Spirit at Its Best

The spirit at its best can laugh
in the face of horror and dance
in the face of death —

[and does]

An Assessment

Much that can be bought
in the world is not needed
and much that is needed
cannot be bought

On the Verge Of

1

On the verge of breaking through
On the verge of creativity finally taking
over the Show that's not a show
On the verge of love turning in hesitation
from walking away
On the verge of peace making more than
just a cameo

On the verge of . . .

2

On the verge of truth escaping from
the false narrative still holding its grip
On the verge of principle having a
permanent seat at the winner's table
On the verge of avarice stepping back
so nobler instincts can take hold
On the verge of the best being spared
from the waste pile

On the verge of . . .

3

On the verge of righting wrongs that have
been waiting long [so long] to be set right

On the verge of justice being present
for the service of all
On the verge of fear moving aside so courage
beyond the passing will come forth
On the verge of minds in needed numbers
opening bravely to the light of old and new

On the verge of . . .

If only . . .

A wish for

And of Humankind

I think of a vehicle thousands of years
old that breaks down again and again
and through all that time its travel
has not been far on the journey that
matters most, and the distance ahead
is so much farther than it has gone
[so far it needs to go] and I think
of humankind as that vehicle
on its way to the Sublime —

Leaving Themselves Behind

. . . as adolescents often do, engaging in something daring when part of a group . . . like crossing a wide body of water or getting from one terrain to another at a dangerous height, navigating a connecting log or narrow bridge, the stability of its structure unknown . . . then one by one, they go — all but one or two . . . those who left for the other side, beckoning whoever stayed behind to follow, but they refuse, fearful of what might happen if they venture to cross . . . and so it is with what often transpires in a dimension of life greater in depth and meaning — those who cross over from the temporal to the eternal of human-being wait for others to make the journey, hoping for them to see what's on the other side — but here it is the reverse of the story above — here, it is the few who cross, and the many who are left behind . . .

[leaving themselves behind]

Landscapes

From around mid-spring till the end of the summer season, landscapers appear year after year at the homes of residents who want their lawns to be cleaned and groomed, arriving in crews to do the work of cutting and trimming and clearing the debris to be taken away and disposed of somewhere (not saying where) keeping the residents happy on that front, giving them nice front lawns that draw compliments from householders nearby and passersby alike, telling them how beautiful their yards are and how they complement the neighborhood and the like, and a thought comes to mind while driving through such an environment about the inner landscape and what it takes to clean it up, get it in order and keep it that way, musing on the difference between the outer and the inner, this being the absence of crews to help with the internal landscaping, leaving it to everyone to do or not do, creating refinement and beauty within on one's own or going the way of neglect, letting the weeds grow wild in the gardens of the soul —

Side Roads and Back Roads

Cliché and Sentimentality — generating
traffic [thick traffic] always bumper to
bumper, manifesting without end on the
main streets of life — its side roads and
back roads never crowded, accommodating
lone travellers in Originality's service
making their way toward getaways far
from the roads most travelled and paths
ever beaten, on to mountainous regions
rich in spiritual treasure, to be mined
and delivered to the world —

Never a Chorus

It is never a chorus that gives a new melody to the world . . .

Coming always from the solo voice

The Way It Is

You can't create a lot if you don't
think a lot, and you can't think
a lot if you're not alone a lot
and you can't be alone a lot unless
you are willing to forgo much
of what those who never create
make much of their lives about —

[Lights out]

A Difference

Many want to tell others about
themselves through times that
are special in their lives; about
lasting effects and impressions
of experiences they've had, of
indelible moments to be savored;
things they'll long remember
while the artist of sufficient depth,
power, gifts, goes about his work
[his business] creating things
that people yet to be born will
one day long remember —

When Disposed to Thought

However much you manage to read
there'll always be more interesting
material to give your mind to that
you will never get around to perusing
let alone finishing, but if you're disposed
to thinking and [even more] want to
probe further and deeper into the
universe of thought [your own thought]
it's important and in multiple ways,
better to spend much time observing
the world closely and to think
[truly *think*] about what you see —
and take time for reverie; to daydream —
let the imagination take hold of the
mind for frequent sessions of museful
exercise and varied modes of freestyle;
this, essential if you want your thought
to be colored with creativity, adding
breadth and depth and power to your
mental apparatus, giving it balance . . .

[the left brain, right brain thing] —

Waiting to Delight

Behind a cluster of gray clouds there's a
shade of blue given the eye to see, suggesting
more there to be perceived but for now, the
greater sky of blue is veiled by a darkened
mass of water vapor and dust holding in
place or far enough away to keep from sight
whatever motion might be at work in the
clouds' formation, and then a discernible
break in the troposphere above and in a
time close to soon, the heavens are filled
with blue [a take-your-breath-away blue]
followed by a mind's recording of how often
life is a reflection of this — something fine
[sometimes remarkable], there behind passing
troubles, waiting to delight . . . something better
than what is seen or focused on that is present
though not within range of awareness, and
then it appears — sensed before recognized . . .
the moving of life-clouds away

No Matter What

Among the gifts most bountiful that
Nature holds are the finest examples
that can be received [bestowed]
of a model recovery after some
natural upheaval or catastrophe . . .
no matter what happens in the sphere
of climate that make up the elements
of meteorological extremes, what
follows (and not long after) is an
ecological presence without sign
of chaos or disturbance, tantamount
to nothing ever happening, life in
Nature's realm going along well
and strong (even joyous on the
whole if it were of its way to be so)
keeping it all going, working the day
day after day without complaint

no matter what

Resurrection

In some desert regions of Africa there are
mountains with craters that serve as pools
supplying drinking water for native animals
when the rains come, and the interval
between rainfalls is sometimes long, leaving
the craters dry and the organisms inside them,
able to generate and be sustained for a time
in their natural form from previous rainfalls,
lie dormant during the dry spells, though within
minutes after a downpour they're rejuvenated,
as if being resurrected from the dead —
and so it is with life within the human heart . . .
energies thought to be expired are often
present, but in a state of rest, stirred from
dormancy by some memory or experience,
or an inspiration that triggers their awakening,
infusing the heart with sensations that surprise,
thought never to be felt again, but they still live,
and still teach, gifting again their lessons of old
and some new, to be taken into the inner depths
to arise once more and influence the life in which
they endure, that they are a living part of, again.

II

On a Hill

Looking out, taking in;

the sky, holding so much

in its space, mirroring

the infinite

Like a Symphony

Raging, howling, like a Grand Nature
Symphony . . . a snowstorm, fierce in both
sound and visual fury gusting in varying
tempos with decibels rising to crescendo
after crescendo, peaking and subsiding
only to peak again with striking power
and majesty, as beautiful as the best of
peaceful hours through the days of autumn,
spring or summer, the storm then easing
in its force, winding to its end with a
growing calm as many great works that
have stormed a symphony hall have done —

Witness to Perfection

. . . Beethoven on the radio — a performance of one of his symphonies [the mighty Fifth] and the windows are open in the room where the broadcast is sounding, their shades three-quarters of the way down, covering the top panes and half of the bottom screens,
the quarters without cover fully exposed to the outer air, the windows set beside each other sharing the same wall and the wind is moving the shades together in a broad range of vertical motion with various degrees of force and height, the waves of air flowing in synchrony with the different measures of volume and intensity of the music, the wind and music (here) creating a union of harmony rising to the scale of perfection, birthing a realization of how fine Nature goes with art and art with Nature sometimes, giving pause to one to reflect upon in appreciation of the profound —

Nature Jazz

What sounds can be produced in the wilds
of Nature — her winged and feathered creatures
speaking to each other; chirping and singing
in response to one another, creating a variety
of bird calls and bird songs in rhythms
Stravinsky would be proud of; percussive
as the brilliant Bartók (he too [I believe]
would be impressed) . . . Sounds with meters
of an alluring nature more interesting than
any chatter to be encountered on any city
street — a gift, surely, to anyone who sees it
(hears it) as such . . . one of Nature's many —

To Take It All In

Holding still and quiet, rapt in a poetic
mood, letting the world stay with you,
be with you, there where you are
and as you are, free of all expectation,
accepting at that moment what is
happening and what is next to come
with a state of mind [of being] the
same as though nothing were occurring
or to be, filling you with a profound peace
pregnant with strength and energy,
letting it all go to take it all in —

The Poet's Birth of Awakening

. . . when words take him by the
mind as a guardian by the hand
and open a world inexhaustible
of meaning and power and truth —

As Ancient Palms

Leaves

      floating down a

           stream like palms

of ancient hands

      cuffing beams

           of sunlight

When Crowded and Empty

Sometimes when streets are
crowded it seems like no one
is there and when empty,
like all are there walking
on cement clouds above
the sweep of time —

Oceans

Oceans kissing the coasts of lands around
the globe, giving them their identity, their
definition, at the oceans' mercy of being
swallowed by their waters as examples
throughout the geological history of
the earth will show — lands existing by
the oceans' generosity, and what lies in
their depths, perhaps to one day surface
or resurface, changing the geography
of shorelines taking their place before
the sun, raised to a world of air and
light from watered tombs that once
served as playgrounds for sea animals
now with fewer toys to play with —

Thrill of a Youth Time

They saw the fish swimming in the creek —
a good twelve pounds or more . . . a fresh-
water bass moving slowly, then gradually
picking up speed, the fisher boys running
with their lures dangling at the end of their
rods casting them in front of it, but the bass
refused to bite, going about its business
navigating the creek without a show of
concern, ignoring the attempts being
made on its life . . . they tried to take it
from under its head, its torso, near its
tail, anywhere they could get their hooks
into it, without success (what they would
have given for a net!) their young hearts
pounding with excitement, wanting to
catch the biggest fish they'd ever seen
on its way to the lake . . . the thrill they
experienced in those moments of exhilaration
has rarely been matched in the years since
that day has past, despite the great
disappointment of the bass's escape . . .

(Today as I reminisce, I'm glad it got away)

Just Thought to Mention

The passing of cars driving
through puddles in the street
is a strange sound in the eve
of a New England January

Touch of Seasons

A stream of wind joining the clouds,
playing its part in placing the last
precipitation of winter according
to calendar, on steps and walkway
and road, meeting together the
mixture of snow and light rain
continuing on in the early hours
of the new season, falling at the
same instant on grounds both near
and distant where feet will step
and tires roll round as before,
ready for travellers to enter
the dawn with a glow of light
up over yonder also in the mix —

Looking Up

Looking up while turning for a moment
away from thought, I notice on the cover
of the ceiling light, dust in the design of
a web connected to the blades of the fan
connected to the light, looking like a spider's
been at work, but no — just threads of
dust spun by the fan creating a design
of something simple, not important,
but interesting —

(I've always been a fan of such things)

Still Light There

Times there are when a room determined
by all corporal sight to be pitch dark will
still have light, like when lying in bed awake
not being able to sleep but able to *think*
(and not really wanting to sleep), the mind
alight with conscious energy, sometimes
creating anew, other times gleaning a
different perspective on musings of old,
or bringing opposing concepts together
and gaining fresh insight into their nature;
the light and sometimes flame that can't
be extinguished —

When Sometimes Alone

Time of being alone is now and again
like being in a spiritual rain, washing
away any elements of baseness or
corruption that may have been
gathered from the worldly wing of
the world, and followed on occasion
by a blessing, a fortunate addition
of settling down to a feast of creativity
prepared by the Muses or whatever
description one chooses to give of that
wondrous power that is the greatest gift
that any spirit could possibly know
when sometimes alone —

Different Measure

The best and worst of days are measured
in the main by many according to the state
of weather they're experiencing [or such
being a prominent factor in the equation],
but the artist has a different gauge by which
to measure, having to do with the way the
creative flow is going; whether the mind
and spirit are attuned with the power that
towers above all other, and if yes, to what
degree . . . and the best days of all are when
the strongest that power can be experienced
is in play, and the dreariest when it is silent
[the only kind of quiet the artist truly dreads]
and time does more than fly when the greater
force is delivering, and goes ever so slowly
when nothing arrives on the days that are
set aside for creative work, and nothing
creative is produced —

[the scale by which the artist measures the day]

Before the Flow

For spiritual riches

    to stream forth

(come through)

    there must be breakage

    before the flow

       . . . . .

So Much Left Out

Never short of astonishing when reflecting
on early years and observing now in later
years, the impartments of 'authority figures'
to the young; how many truths/realities
they leave out in their pronouncements of
what the world and life are about and given
their demeanor of confidence, revealing how
unaware they are of all they've failed to
consider, not reflected upon; so much they
never figured out but they say what's what
about this and that, and a thinking mind
inclined to paying attention, listening carefully
to what's being said has question after question,
realizing that nothing close to a thorough
examination has preceded the statements
being made on the subjects addressed, so
much left out [never thought about], but
the talk goes on and the certainty is long
and the confidence is tall and the void
between error and truth, illusion and reality
deepest and widest of all —

The Baby Shower

Drawing people of all sorts
bringing presents of all sorts
with expressions of all sorts
and emotions of some sorts
a baby on its way, soon to be
born drawing sustenance from
the womb of a mother to be,
still sorting things out with
love lighting through the gaze
of apprehension

Odds to Wonder

At the racetrack with his two-year
old son and mother of the child
sitting next to him, a man watches
another two-year old with excitement
rounding the track, one that he bet on
making good this time — a winner
crossing the finish line first . . . what
are the odds that he will ever have
the same focus or measure of interest
in the development of his two-year old
progeny there by his side, to go as well
the challenging track of life . . .

Too Much to Handle

People look to settle down, decide to
marry and sometimes one mate finds
the other too much to handle, then
kids arrive and become too much to
handle and as life goes on [moves along]
it all gets too much to handle, the
matters to deal with inside and outside
the household oftentimes unmanageable
then the ride [the crazy ride] comes
to an end, and the time seems to have
passed so fast but while passing
seemed so slow and then checkout time
arrives, with odds and ends and more
odds to clean up, to get in order . . .
leaving for others to handle —

Of Birth and Death

At the entrance of your life there are
people around you and [for most] at the
exit too, but at both ends there is the same
unknowing, for at the beginning, awareness
is not of the development to know or inform
you as to what's going on; too young, you are
[too raw], to have the lowdown on the show
of blood and tears and all [the breathing
just barely begun] and at the other end
[the exit end] you're in a state outside
of knowing the goings-on of the living,
as the gestures and small talk and maybe
some big talk sound on, and the sounds of
emotions behind the shedding of tears
more likely than not, like at the starting
end but for different reasons [from different
emotions] and then there's the chance
[always the chance] that in the minds of
some present at the funeral/eulogy or the
like, strikes the phrase "Good Riddance"
while getting ready for your six feet under
when not long before you were six feet over
and moving about [breathing above] and
your time now over without knowing it

[just running out] —

No Longer Step

How many there are
who stay or go in lockstep
with the dead who
no longer step

Well Well Well

They want you to talk well and
to look well, dress well and move
well and to play well and sit well
[with others] and to work well
[especially for others] and to wear
well and go along well, fit in
well and obey well and to adjust
well and be all in all agreeable
to much that virtue and integrity
would find disagreeable —

Those who don't live well in the
principled sense —

With Minds Closed

They — with their invitations to
liberal dialogue;
They — with their professed advocacy
for impartial discussion;
They — with their proud touting of
open-door policy for an honest
exchange of ideas;
They — who preach the sacrosanctness
of free speech and declare their
unwavering support for its protection
as their minds remain closed —

Killing Santa Claus

There are those who boast that from
an early age they no longer believed
in Santa Claus, yet tell them truths
about the human condition that they
don't think about, never contemplate
(just don't want to hear) and they
look at you like you've just stolen
their belief in Santa Claus away
from them —

Pet Watch

I watch you walking on all fours and
ponder a time when sapiens were not yet,
and what they have given up in their gain
of standing on all twos, standing erect
and proud, though the clouds of missteps
are in the air, consequence closing in
with traits of man still dragging on the
ground despite his sometimes show of
genius . . . the weight of his fear, for
instance, leaving imprints on the trail
of his journey —

Complacent Trance

Seems like humankind is ever on its way
to nodding off no matter what crashes
into it from within or without — it gets
a jolt, receives its shock but then retreats
soon after the uninvited wake-up, back
into a complacent not-quite-with-it trance
near to slumber, not planning for the
next crash or thinking about the last —

The Perilous Wait

Like deaf beings waiting for the shot
in the air to sound that's been fired;
like blind beings waiting for the flash
of green light to begin that's been flashing,
waiting until it is gone . . .

O Man . . . what are you waiting for?
Living as if you're deaf and blind to the
urgency of your plight . . .

CHANGE

Change . . . yes — another time for hordes
of enthusiasts to declare they've had enough
of the status quo . . . they now demand *change* —

Hot and ready to go; to get it done, to make
it happen . . .

Ahh . . . . but when the price is realized, when
the reality of what it will take to do what they
have in mind sets in, the scale of work they'll
need to execute to succeed and subsequent efforts
involved to hold the gains that are achieved,

Note how many of these soldiers for change
give up, head for the hills — the lifelong
commitment to sustain the dream just too much,
too great a sacrifice, and so

Goes another gleam of hope, another failed
endeavor . . .

Ever the disappointment of what was launched
with impassioned energy and determination
turning to nothing

(or worse)

Over the Rest

Ambitionists working the day
wanting a leg up and an arm up
and a head up over the next
go-getter and the rest who want
to be of the worldly best, getting
to whatever it is they're after or
getting done or close to getting
done or trying to get done in the
long run or short run for nothing
or near to nothing, scrambling about
for the score of no value

for the dream of no value

for the prize of no value

managing to get through another day,
fooling themselves and other players
of the game, keeping the grand illusion
of the not so very grand in play —

Empty Beneath the Sun

You hear them through phones, across from
tables, over airwaves, in hallways, through
open doors and windows; voices of a tone
that smacks of complacency, of being too
comfortable, signifying something about
those to whom they belong [the too-pleased-
with-themselves crowd]; more self-satisfied
than their stature based solely on merit would
warrant . . . and one thinks again while given
a reminder, of how much of human society is
mired in mediocrity as the voices sound on
without a hint of care as if all were being
taken care of, no need to be concerned with
anything unpleasant, or bothered about
negatives born of faulty action and inaction
growing in consequence when all is well
with them and their bubbled worlds as
the world falls deeper into a human-made
hell . . . voices like rafts in pools, empty
beneath the sun

Ripe for the Breaking

Horrible stories come over the news about
humans doing horrible things; people snapping,
having a breakdown and then all hell breaks
loose from them and [unfortunately] let loose
upon others who are often unsuspecting and
chosen at random, and then one wonders . . .
how many are out there going about their
days, their business [their lives] barely
holding it together, as close as one can get
to the breaking point without breaking
and no one around them having a hint of it,
and perhaps some of the ready-to-exploders
too not having a clue right up to the moment
of fracture, as unaware of the danger of how
easily it could go badly for them as for those
close by who at any time could meet a sorry
end from an onslaught of madness breaking
out [breaking free] and would it be an absurdity
to wonder if the whole human world itself
might be in the same predicament, for now
holding together but living with numerous
cracks, not yet broken, but ripe [so ripe]
for the breaking . . .

Still Searching For

Known are those who follow wiseless
sets of rules formulated by wiseless views
carted around by the wiseless, denying
all visits to the funny farm where no one
ever laughs and children ride by in
marked cars preparing for the mocking
of their lives yet searching for a place
in the world that man has yet to betray,
and someone from the "Look at me!"
crowd who will show himself to be
more than just a Wow most hollow,
eyeing no looking glass made of plastic,
wanting only the kind that will draw
blood from the slightest cut —

For Ray

A ray of light for Ray sitting on his
stool ordering another drink, the
morning sunbeam coming in through
the blinds, lighting the bar with a
glow of golden yellow tending to
his wounds as he muses on days
gone by filled with hopes and promise,
the bartender bringing him his order —
liquid fire in a glass . . .

the day just getting started

Good Time Benny

Lost all he had — his family, his friends,
his fortune from a thousand drinks too many —
no one tried to stop him [to help him] . . .
spoke nary a word of the harm he was
doing to himself inside and out and the
inevitable ending he would meet so long
as he was buying ["Drinks for everyone!"]
with laughs and poor jokes and ruffles on
the head and pats on the back with nobody
watching his back, till one day a liver gave
out followed by a heart that were Benny's,
and the Good Time Benny Show came to
an end and when news of his passing was
heard, a desire within the regular bar crowd
was stirred for a farewell drink, one last
round in remembrance of Benny, but
no one offered to put up the money —

Fantasy Meets Fantasy

One said she was tired of all the games, the
hustles, the shallow nonsense often encountered
in the standard dating venues to find
a mate; she wanted more from the partner
she was looking for —

Another said he was tired of all the games, the
hustles, the shallow nonsense often encountered
in the standard dating venues to find
a mate; he wanted more from the partner
he was looking for —

Both believing they had better to offer than
they possessed but when they met, each had
little more to present to the other than what
they'd learned from the games, the hustles,
the shallow nonsense fresh in their minds,
straight from the venues they patronized
and their assumptions of being more than
they are, not founded on anything substantive
[nothing close to real], like dreaming a
trust fund was left to them, would be there
when they wanted it, though such was
never given . . . (just figments of imaginations
coupled with sentience void of self-awareness) —

Air Speak

What some have the
mouth for [the tongue for]
haven't the mind for
the heart for
the will for
the strength for
the courage for
the spirit for

(as the talk goes on . . .)

Not a Note

Seated at the same table near the front of the stage, rarely missing a show, the stern critic critiquing the bands of musicians passing through the nightclub, rating their performance while tapping his chin with his finger (sometimes fingers) quick to declare who was good and who wasn't (who had the talent ["the chops"] and who didn't) — not a doubt in his eyes of the truth of his assessment, the value of his judgment; sitting there, night after night taking mental notes on the merits of those who were hitting the beats and playing the notes . . . the self-appointed critic, who couldn't play a note —

Once Budding King

Finding the man face down on the
trash-filled ground, the junkyard dog
ripping at his trousers, the air growing
cold, chilling the arteries of the old sot
spitting blood and rage over the life
that he has led; for the mess he's made
of it, and of himself — the wretch of a
man that he'd become, leaving him lost
and broken . . . the once budding king
throwing in the towel, raising the
white flag, now face to the ground,
losing a face that never really was —

Winking at Shadows

Those thousand and two lessons of ugly
learned at the beauty parlor have served you
well in your private hell — leathered hands
of spotted brown and protruding vessels
of blue, selecting your evening gown taken
from the nursery stitching scenes of metabolic
heat shaping your next thought of color-by-
senses . . . traces of beaus still on the dresser
winking at shadows dancing with memories
of lost youth painfully unforgotten, the pull
of gravity now the torturous enemy mocking
the dimension of your life [your being]
that could have made this all as nothing
now shrivelled to nothing, joining the all
too many in number who faced the horror
of too late   too late —

Suicides

Climbing the walls of midnight
fleeing whispers cutting to the bone,
dreams awaiting their next fate in
frames of sired urgency when only
the most serious things can get you
to laugh out loud, turning from offerings
of a pale glory and breaches of old
finally succumbing to surrender where
trumpets are heard when only flutes
are playing, and the cast of eyes that see
nothing but what is wed to the unseen
slipping moon days into the shadows
of lost peaks, believing the sky will
never abandon and the winds of truth
will always stream on at the closing
of death's hour —

Something Lost

In striving to get ahead, people often
get ahead of themselves, leaving their
best behind; that sorry tune sounding
in the back of their minds "Whatever
happened to . . . " going from happening
to shallow happening, losing their direction,
the light of perception, wondering some-
where along the way why they're so
disheartened and why virtually everything
they've achieved, what they have worked
for so long to acquire and supposed to
have wanted begins to look empty and
void of meaning; an absence of something
most valuable to their lives now being felt,
getting lost in the hustle of striving to get
ahead while leaving their best behind —

Of Lives Taken

Many fill their time with what others do to
fill their time or could easily do with their
time, requiring no special skill or power of
mind to speak of, keeping themselves busy
but not accomplishing much, and one wonders
if they will ever get to the experience of *life*,
needing to first slow their pace, then stop —
(then) step away from what has taken them
in a direction away from the sublimities of the
infinite to the opposites that have taken their
lives [which they've allowed to be taken]
and get to what is more by doing less of what
indulges the transient [much less] and more
[far more] of the internal work that frees
the power and light that make all investment
in the ascension of human life worth every
effort and sacrifice —

Before the Parting

On planes of domesticity many a promise has been taken down, potentials unfulfilled — but not in the usual way [like wolf upon prey]; here, it is a reversal of order [like prey upon wolf] . . . something of creativity, originality, the power of invention, lost — gone to the taming prison of some 'till-death-do-us-part'ness — the dying here beginning before the parting —

The Finest $ Can Buy

Customers going in and out the door,
coming now for near to forty years, greeting
employees and the owner who's also head
baker, long knowing that part of his job
is listening to buyers standing before the
counter telling him stories about their
employments and families and hobbies
and other matters while waiting for
their orders of breads and cakes and pies
(sometimes the finest wedding cake money
can buy) and he obliges masterfully with his
skills in the culinary trade, and a refinement
long practiced of feigned interest in the
chatter of his customers through many days
of banging the dough and ringing up the dough;
the business sound and stable, as patrons enter
and exit the door with what they came for . . .
the baker keeping the air-dance going with
comestible wares of the tangible —

Grand Misunderstanding

Father/Businessman: "The world is passing you by."

Son/Philosopher: "No, I am passing by the world."

Only Man

The sun lights not for money
The rain falls not for money
The birds sing not for money
The bees work not for money
The flowers bloom not for money
The rivers flow not for money
The harvests grow not for money . . .

Only man does   for money

Up or Down

Things happen as they happen
as you just happen to be breathing
at this moment in the stream of time,
looking to what is beyond time
or to be taken by time to what is
hardly worth the ride —

Dead of Life

Where nothing will sing
Where nothing will dance
Where truth refuses to sign
life certificates;
Where the hour has lost its minutes
and the minutes refuse their seconds;
Where love has been replaced with the
lust for comforts and carefully drawn safeness,
and the dead of noise has forced the
hand of youth

Here life has no presence
Here death has the upper hand
[the cold, coarse hand] wrapped
around the heart of spirits
gasping for the air of true life

No Other

In the profound there is love like no other —
In the profound there is beauty like no other —
In the profound there is wisdom like no other —
In the profound there is courage like no other —
And awareness like no other
And generosity like no other
And humor like no other
And serenity like no other
And intensity like no other
And *life* like no other

                        no other

                                no other

                                      . . . . .

Offering to the Young

Get to work early in life (to the inner work)
so you can start building your worth early
(yes, it has to be built) and learn when to say
no, and keep your distance from who and what
are only about show and can be nothing but a
hindrance to the realization of your goals,
and stay conscious of the fact that your time
is only for a time and only fools waste it
(so many waste a lifetime of it) and be as
generous a guest as you can be to this world,
entering with nothing though doing your best
to leave it your best on the way to the exit,
and don't be discouraged by the countless follies
and injustices you will encounter on the journey
but do what you can to mitigate them (it is all
anyone can do) and stay true to the best that
is in you (that is of you) . . .

this, a solemn wish for you —

Saving Grace

For all the mayhem in the world
one is born into, some determine at
some point in time that in spite of it
they'll somehow find a way come
what may, whatever the cost, to
reach something; to discover or
create something that nothing of all
the madness that permeates much of
the manmade goings-on of this world
can claim . . . and it will smile back,
grin with delight as if to say to the
mayhem and triggers of its manifests,
"This, you cannot have . . . It shall
be kept away from your grip, where
the one who has made his way to
me can find solace and meaning"
transcendent of all earthly ills and
confusions, and be a saving grace —

Words

Words that bring it home
Words that see it through
Words that dance in darkness
and sing before light
Words that breathe hope into despair
Words that corner the prize
Words that set thought to flight
Words that impassion
Words that liberate
Words of the power to raise life

Words ever moving, ever saying,
ever living

An Answer

A poet was asked if he loves what he does;
he said, "It is what I do."

"Yes, but do you love it? Could you imagine
living without mining your poetry?" He said,
"It is what I do."

"But do you *love* it, really *love it*? . . ." He replied,
"I can only answer in this way:

"When it does more than I expected, when it
reveals more than I thought it ever could;
when it takes me for a time to regions of mind
and heart and soul I thought I could never go,
then even love for it plays no part, for it is beyond
even that — the calmful ecstasy of the transcendent . . .
it is the only time I am sure that a connection
to the poetry of life has been achieved."

A Place for One

A place to go   where no one is there
A place to be   where no one is there
A place to feel   where no one is there
A place to think   where no one is there
A place to work   where no one is there
A place to create   where no one is there
A place to cultivate where no one is there

The best of the harvest then willed to all —

Cannot Erase

Let youth slip away . . . let age

proceed to a winter's gray and

take away . . . . take away

. . . . so long as the work of the
Eternal has been done

      which

            nothing

of time can erase.

ABOUT THE AUTHOR

Carroll Blair is an award-winning author of more than twenty books. His work has been well endorsed and commendably reviewed, as illustrated by the following commentary from Midwest Review, which proclaimed, *"The poetic expression of Carroll Blair is both unique and compelling. Using word images like the strokes of a painter's brush, Blair creates a resonating recognition that is the mark of a master poet."*
He is an alumnus of the Boston Conservatory and lives in Massachusetts.

www.ingramcontent.com/pod-product-compliance
Lightning Source LLC
Chambersburg PA
CBHW030000050426
42451CB00006B/68